I Need to Win! Tips for Kids on Good Sportsmanship
by Nadine Briggs and Donna Shea
Copyright © 2017 How to Make and Keep Friends, LLC

Published by How to Make & Keep Friends, LLC
Illustrated by Ryan Flynn

ISBN-13: 978-0997280845
ISBN-10: 0997280840

Before we get into talking about good sportsmanship, we want you to know that we already think you are a great person. Every kid that we have ever met has lots of terrific qualities.

Some kids have a little extra difficulty with becoming too competitive. This means you like to win a lot and get frustrated when you don't.

Some kids have trouble with playing fairly or being a good sport. You may know this is true for you or an adult has told you this is something you need to improve. Having difficulty with sportsmanship skills does not mean that you are a bad person.

This workbook includes tips and strategies you can try to make winning and losing easier for you so that playing with friends will be more fun!

WHAT YOU WILL NEED:

 Your brain ready to become a good sport

 A pencil to write down ideas.

 A healthy snack is always nice!

WE HAVE A QUESTION FOR YOU.

Do you think that being COMPETITIVE is a bad thing? Not necessarily.

Let's look at the dictionary definition of competitive.

COMPETITIVE *(adjective)*

1. Of, relating to, or characterized by competition
   a. Synonyms: ruthless, aggressive, fierce
2. As good as or better than others

In other words, being competitive is when you try to win at something. It can sometimes mean wanting to win no matter what! Being super competitive doesn't sound as though it is the friendliest way to be, does it? Being too competitive might be stopping you from having or keeping good friends.

3

However, there are times when being VERY competitive is expected. Many things in our world are based on being super competitive.

DO YOU KNOW WHAT SOME OF THOSE MIGHT BE?

- Professional sports;

- The Olympics; and

- Companies that sell products

CAN YOU THINK OF ANY OTHERS?

 _____

 _____

 _____

There are also times or situations when being SOMEWHAT competitive is expected:

- Participating in a team or individual sport;

- Applying to schools or other places that have limited spaces; and

- Official competitions around a particular skill (dance, cooking, running).

CAN YOU THINK OF ANY OTHERS?

_____

_____

Competition can be a good thing when it helps us strive to do better. You can still be a good sport, even when competing.

Then there are times when being competitive is not expected and can cause problems. Some examples are:

- ⚾ Always trying to be or go first;

- ⚾ Winning at any cost (even cheating);

- ⚾ Putting down a team member if their skills are not as good as yours;

- ⚾ Blaming another player or players if your team loses; or

- ⚾ Arguing and fighting during games that are meant to be friendly or just for fun;

And a few more...

- 🏀 Complaining a lot when the schedule changes or recess is over, and there isn't time to finish a game;

- 🏀 Bragging loudly about how great you are at a game or sport; and

- 🏀 Not allowing someone else to play on your team because you think they aren't good enough or will cause your team to lose.

Can you think of any other situations when it does not work well to be competitive?

- 🏀 _____

- 🏀 _____

- 🏀 _____

Draw or color what **YOUR** brain thinks or how your body responds when you are feeling competitive.

I Need to Win!: Tips for Kids on Good Sportsmanship

UNDERSTANDING GOOD SPORTSMANSHIP

Why is good sportsmanship such a big deal? Being a good sport is one of the most important things you can do to be a good friend, classmate or teammate.

If winning or losing becomes more important than friendship or playing nicely with others; you might find yourself being left out of games or playing alone at recess. Making poor sportsmanship choices might cause other kids to think it is not fun to play with your or be on a team with you.

HERE ARE SOME EXAMPLES OF POOR SPORTSMANSHIP CHOICES:

- Mean insults, putdowns or "trash talk;"

- Teasing or calling another player names;

- Acting as though you are better than everyone else;

- Pointing out or making fun of another player's mistakes;

- Cheating or not playing by the rules; and

- Putting your hands on anyone in anger. (If you feel like you might hurt someone, try pressing your hands together as though you are pushing yourself away, or just walk away and take a break from the activity.

AND A FEW MORE...

- ⚽ Changing the rules for your own benefit;

- ⚽ Frequent claims of "it's not fair!";

- ⚽ Debating about "getting out" in a game;

- ⚽ Having tantrums or throwing things after getting out;

- ⚽ Getting upset over a mistake;

- ⚽ Refusing to play or trying something new;

- ⚽ Arguing instead of working things out;

- ⚽ Wanting everything your own way; or

- ⚽ Seeking revenge or being aggressive.

FILL IN ANY OTHER POOR SPORTMANSHIP CHOICES YOU CAN THINK OF:

Being a poor sport can cause you to lose friends. It's important to learn and remember that winning is not more important than your friendships!

If you have a friend that is being a bad sport, you can tell them that you only want to play fair and have fun or you will play with someone else for a while.

TIPS ON BEING A GOOD SPORT

Tip #1: Play by the rules
All games and activities have specific instructions and rules.

- Reviewing the rules before playing can help to avoid confusion or disagreements.

- If there is a disagreement on the rules, a good plan is to check the rules. People may have different ways of playing a game. The internet is a good place to find official rules (ask an adult before going online).

- However, if everyone agrees to change a rule, then it is okay to use it

- A good rule to use is every time you play a game is to play **strategically** (making the best move available) instead of **revengefully** (getting even with someone for something they did to you in the game). There are fewer arguments when everyone just makes the most strategic move.

Tip #2: Be brave enough to try something new

Trying a new game or activity might make you nervous or worried.

- It's okay to ask how to play or let others know you are not sure.

  - Be willing to give it a try.

- You might decide to watch first if you are not sure if you want to play.

- It only takes 10 seconds of courage to try something new. Or decide to try one new thing, one time, for one minute.

- When you try a new game or play something that isn't your favorite, you are showing other kids that you want to be friends.

Tip #3: Be good at both winning AND losing

- When you have lost a game, you can say "good game" or congratulate the winner.

- If you win, you can say something encouraging to the person or team who lost (see the appendix for what you might say).

- Bragging about winning or complaining about losing is not showing good sportsmanship.

- Know the difference between friendly "trash talk" that is meant to be funny and putting someone else down. EXAMPLE: "You are sooooo going down!" is fun. "You aren't very good at this game, are you?" is an insult.

- We have never met a kid who enjoys it when another kid says "na-nah na-nah boo-boo" while playing, so don't say it.

15

- Many games are games of luck and not games of skill. You win some. You lose some. It won't matter how well you know how to play the game. Usually, any games where you have to draw cards or roll dice to move are games based on luck.

- If you are feeling upset about losing, it can help to walk away and take a break. Try a few deep breaths to calm down before saying anything.

- Even though you might be upset about losing, don't accuse the other players of cheating.

I Need to Win!: Tips for Kids on Good Sportsmanship

- If you think cheating happened, but no one else saw it, calmly ask to go over the rules again or speak to the coach in private.

- Cheating to win is not a real win. If someone cheats a lot, you can choose to either let it go or not play anymore.

- If you lose at tag or another game where you are "out" for a while, try the "walk of out." The "walk of out" is when you make a dramatic exit with funny and exaggerated steps. It can make getting "out" fun!

Whether you have won or lost a game, giving a friendly "high five" demonstrates good sportsmanship. A friendly high five is one that uses the right about of muscle and not one that leaves your opponent with a stinging hand! You can practice how hard to "high five" with an adult if you are not sure!

List some things you can say if you win:

_____   _____

_____   _____

_____   _____

List some things you can say if you lose:

_____   _____

_____   _____

_____   _____

If you do become upset with your performance or your team's performance, here are some things that you can do instead of getting angry or complaining:

- 🏈 Practice;

- 🏈 Ask your coach how you can improve and then practice that;

- 🏈 Offer to help your teamates;

- 🏈 Brainstorm with your team or coach to come up with some new strategies; and

- 🏈 Make sure you have enough rest, eat a healthy diet and stay hydrated. These things can help you keep control of your emotions.

Tip #4: Be able to laugh at yourself or shrug it off when you make a mistake

- Sometimes things may not go as expected

- Being able to laugh at your mistakes is a great demonstration of being a good sport.

- It's important to remember that EVERYONE makes mistakes now and then.

- Make it fun and "fail with flair." If you make a mistake or get out, be a little goofy and laugh it off or just shrug your shoulders with a "who cares" and try again!

- Shrugging things off does not mean that you should grumpily state that you are not good at whatever you are playing.

- "Do-overs" can be used for mistakes and can be a terrific way to prevent arguments too!

Tip #5: Be an optimist and positive thinker

- Part of being a good sport is being cheerful even if you are unable to do everything you want to do.

- Another part is making the best of it when something goes wrong.

- It can be helpful to remember that there are many good things to be happy about in life and that winning and losing isn't everything.

- Think about if winning a game is that important or not. Think of a scale of 1-5. Where does losing rank for you

List some things in your life that you are happy about:

_____

_____

_____

_____

_____

_____

Tip #6: Cheer for your friends' successes

- When a friend does well at something, show that you are happy for him or her (even if you feel a little jealous.) Do this by telling them that you are excited for them and say, "Congratulations!"

- It is important to remember that the success belongs to your friend at that moment, so that is not the time to share a success story of your own. This can be called trying to "one-up" a friend.

- What if the success was yours? Would you want your friend to be happy for you?

Example: Your friend just won a big shiny trophy. What could you say?

_____

_____

_____

_____

_____

_____

Tip #7: Be willing to change the plan if needed

- Unexpected things sometimes happen that might ruin your plans.

- Being a good sport means using your creative thinking to come up with an alternative plan.

- Sometimes the only solution to ruined plans is for you to accept that it happened and there is nothing you can do about it.

Example: You have planned to go to a big amusement park, and when you wake up, it is raining. What do you do?

_____

_____

_____

_____

_____

_____

_____

Tip #8: Understand and accept that it is impossible to have your way every time.

- A good sport does not demand their way all the time.

- If a friend is playing differently than you are, don't tell them that they are doing it wrong.

- Be flexible, open-minded and willing to accept a friend's idea or an adult's decision.

- Allow everyone's ideas to have a turn to play.

- Try saying "how about we?" when offering an idea. "How about we" is friendlier and more cooperative than "you have to."

- Choosing games can solve problems if things get stuck (see the appendix for some examples of choosing games).

- Remember that there are no "better" ideas, only "different" ideas.

"HERE'S ONE FOR THE TOP!"

Tip #9: Work together to make games and activities you play at recess to be fun for everyone.

In general, it's a good idea to review the rules with the other players before you start to play. Going over the rules will prevent arguments and help new kids learn a game. Here are some general rules for playing these common games at recess:

TAG

- When you're out, stay out.

- Tag with one hand, flat palm on the arm or back.

- No shoving others with your hands or body .

- Don't try to tag kids who aren't playing.

- Stay within the boundary if there is one.

- As a group, talk about if there is a "base" and if there is a time limit for being on base.

FOUR SQUARE

- 🏀 When you get out, don't argue or complain. It holds up the game, and you have less time to play.

- 🏀 Get back in line quickly and don't cut the line.

- 🏀 Know the particular rules that the kids in your school use to play. There are different variations.

- 🏀 Hit the ball underhand. Spiking it makes it hard for anyone else to return the ball and isn't nice.

- 🏀 If it's on a line or you are unsure of who was out, use a do-over.

Soccer, Baseball, Basketball, etc...

- ⚽ Organized games all have specific rules. Make sure you know what they are and if you don't, ask.

- ⚽ Don't run in and grab the ball to run away with it. If you want to play, make sure you join in the right way, by saying "I want to play too. Which team can I be on?"

- ⚽ If you play one of these organized sports on a real team in school or for your town, recess is not the place to be super competitive. Give everyone a chance, even if they are not the greatest of players.

Tip #10: Play on Playground Safely and Fairly

You should also practice good sportsmanship and play nicely with friends on the playground.

★ Be safe. You should play on the playground structures the way it is intended. For example, don't climb the slide the wrong way.

★ Don't block other people on the equipment, move out of the way if other kids want to get past you.

★ Make sure everyone has a fair turn on community equipment.

★ If it is a public playground, make sure to watch out for younger kids.

★ Include everyone in the game who wants to play.

★ Ask any kids who are nearby if they want to play, they might feel too shy to come over.

★ Playing with new friends can make things more fun!

FACTS ABOUT SPORTSMANSHIP

Fact #1: Good Sports find ways to include everyone and have fun!

Fact #2: Most of the time, playing together is a social event and meant to be friendly and fun. Every game is not about winning a trophy.

Fact #3: You can be a good sport, no matter what age you are. Older kids can set a good example for younger kids. You can encourage younger children to play fairly and just have fun.

Fact #4: People who are good sports are more fun to play with and be around.

Fact #5: We guarantee that people who are good sports will have more friends and more fun!

SPORTSMANSHIP QUIZ circle either ✓ or ✗

You ran a race that you lost and shook hands with the person who won.

 Your friend struck out at bat and lost the game, and the rest of the team called him a loser.

You were called off-sides while playing soccer and complained to the referee.

 During a game of dodge ball, you were hit by the ball, but no one saw it. You still came out of the round.

When you started to lose at a game of checkers, you messed up all the on the board and quit.

 You couldn't level up in your video game, but you said to yourself, "That stinks, but I'll just try to beat the level again."

You were asked to play a game that you do not know how to play and said, "that game is just stupid."

 You are the captain of the kickball team, and you only choose the kids who run the fastest to be on your side.

FINISH

33

WHAT WOULD YOU DO IF...

The coach says the entire team must do the drill over again because some of the players did not listen to the instructions?

_____

_____

_____

_____

Your best friend just beat you in your favorite video game?

_____

_____

_____

_____

You are upset because you have been working hard all season and you didn't play as well as you wanted to in the finals?

_____

_____

_____

_____

You tried out for the school play and didn't get the part you wanted?

_____

_____

_____

_____

WHAT WOULD YOU DO IF...

Your team just won a game
over your biggest rival?

_____

_____

_____

_____

Your friend wants to go first in
a game and, so do you?

_____

_____

_____

_____

WATCH OUT FOR THE "YEAH BUTS!"

 Be careful that you don't get a sneaky case of the Yeah Buts! What are the Yeah Buts? When you are given tons of strategies to help you be a better sport, and you respond with "yeah... but..." followed by why you think it will not work. There are lots of strategies in this book, and we're sure more than a few can help you if you give them a solid try.

Remember, you are in charge of your life and decisions. Think about how you would feel if other kids made fun of your skills, called you a "loser" or blamed you if your team lost. Choosing to be a good sport by managing your thoughts and reactions can be hard work, but it will change your life in very positive and powerful ways.

Everyone is different and will find various tips useful. Pick a few tips to practice, and you will be well on your way to becoming a great sport!

You have the power to make your life happier, be a positive thinker and a great sport, and have lots of kids want to play with you!

REMEMBER: GOOD SPORTS **ALWAYS** WIN!

APPENDIX

Here are some words you can say to be a good winner or loser. Can you think of any others to put in the bubbles?

CHOOSING GAMES

Rock, Paper Scissors

The players count aloud to three, or speak the name of the game "Rock! Paper! Scissors!" while, with each word raising one hand in a fist and swinging it down on the count. On the third count, while saying "Three!" or "Scissors!", the players change their hands into one of three gestures, which they then "throw" by extending it towards their opponent. Variations include a version where players use the fourth count, "Shoot!", before throwing their chosen gesture. There is also another version where the players only shake their hands twice before throwing. Others prefer a five-count cadence by adding "Says Shoot!" before throwing their gesture. The gestures are:

ROCK
represented by a clenched fist

SCISSORS
represented by the index and middle fingers extended and seperated and,

PAPER

represented by an open hand, with fingers connected and horizontal

The object is to select a gesture which defeats that of the opponent. Resolve gestures as follows:

Rock blunts or breaks scissors: **Rock defeats scissors!**

Scissors cut paper: **Scissors defeats paper**

Paper covers or captures rock: **Paper defeats rock**

If Both players choose the same gesture, the game is tied and the players counta and throw again.

Source: http://en.wikipedia.org/wiki/Rock-paper-scissors

I Need to Win!: Tips for Kids on Good Sportsmanship

Flip a Coin

Tossed the coin into the air such that it rotates end-over-end severa times. Either beforehand, or when the coin is in the air, one person calls "heads" or "tails," indicating which side of the coin that person or team is choosing. The other individual or group is assigned the opposite side of the coin. Depending on custom, the coin may be caught and inverted on the back of the hand; or allowed to land on the ground. When the coin comes to rest, the toss is complete, and the person or team who called or was assigned the side facing up is declared the winner. Repeat the toss if the outcome is unclear.

Source: http://en.wikipedia.org/wiki/Coin_flipping

Drawing Straws

Drawing straws is a selection method used by a group to choose one person to do a task when no one has volunteered for it. The same practice could also be used to pick one of the several volunteers should an agreement not be reached. The group leader takes the same number of straws or similar long, cylindrical objects as there are people, and makes sure one of the straws is physically shorter than the rest. The leader then grabs all the straws in his or her fist such that all of them appear to be of the same length. The leader then offers the clenched fist to the group. Each member or player draws a straw from the fist. At the end of the offering, the person with the shortest straw is the one who must do the task.

Source: http://en.wikipedia.org/wiki/Drawing_straws

Eeny, Meeny, Miny, Moe

"Eeny, meeny, miny, moe," (which you can spell several different ways), is a children's counting rhyme used to select a person to be "it." It is one of a large group of similar counting-out rhymes where the child pointed to by the person chanting on the last syllable is counted out.

Source: http://en.wikipedia.org/wiki/Eeny,_meeny,_miny,_moe

Spuds Up

In this game, "spuds" means potatoes, and refers to each person's fists. Standing or sitting in a circle, each person puts his or her fists forward. One person chants "One potato, two potatoes, three potatoes four, five potatoes, six potatoes, seven potatoes, more," with each word pointing to the next spud, going around the circle clockwise. The spud (hand) on which the word "more" is spoken is eliminated, and the player will then place that hand behind his or her back. The chant starts again from the next spud. A player is out when both their spuds (or hands) are eliminated. The game continues until there is only one "spud" left and that person is the winner.

Source: http://en.wikipedia.org/wiki/Selection_methods

Are there any other choosing games you know?

_____

_____

_____

_____

_____

_____

_____

_____

_____

_____

We make every effort to identify original sources for tips that we share. Many ideas are in some form in the public domain. If you are aware of a source for an idea, please let us know, and we will make sure to cite it.

That's it! Thank you so much for reading our book!

We would love to hear what you thought about these tips and how they may have helped you improve your sportsmanship skills. We are also always interested in new ideas from kids that read our books!

Your mom and dad can help you write or email us.

howtomakeandkeepfriends@gmail.com

How to Make and Keep Friends, LLC
P.O. Box 312
Harvard, MA 01451

We would appreciate it if you would take a minute to review our book on Amazon. We learn a great deal from our readers and your comments!

About the Authors

Donna Shea and Nadine Briggs are both accomplished social educators. They each facilitate friendship groups at their respective centers in Massachusetts. Both Nadine and Donna are parents of children with special needs.

Donna and Nadine consult with schools, parent groups, and human service agencies. They are also seasoned public speakers and travel to bring workshops and seminars to schools, conferences, and other venues across the country.

Donna and Nadine are certified in bullying prevention through the Massachusetts Aggression Reduction Center and are creators of the How to Make & Keep Friends Social Success in School initiative to provide classroom training and team building for school systems. Both Nadine and Donna have attained specializations in Foundations of Positive Psychology through the University of Pennsylvania.

We would love to receive your feedback on our books, to speak with you about providing programming in your area, and to keep in touch when new books and materials become available.

Find us on Facebook

Email us at howtomakeandkeepfriends@gmail.com

Also by Nadine and Donna

The updated and revised edition of How to Make & Keep Friends: Tips for Kids to Overcome 50 Common Social Challenges offers social skills and friendship advice presented in an easy to read, reference guide format. Included are simple and immediately actionable tips to navigate everyday social situations that can be challenging, including • How to Join a Group • How to Safely Handle Angry Feelings • Handling Rejection and Exclusion • Working Things Out & Sharing • Being a Good Guest and Host • Playground Success and much more! In this edition, we have added why learning each of these skills is important along with practice questions to inspire discussion and role playing of different social situations with children.

How to Make and Keep Friends: Helping Your Child Achieve Social Success is a how-to manual for parents of children with social challenges. The easy-to-read format outlines common barriers that hinder friendships, provides actionable tips for overcoming those areas of difficulty. The book also includes suggested language for parents to use to support their child during unstructured social interactions. Parents play a vital role in the formation of friendships. How to Make and Keep Friends: Helping Your Child Achieve Social Success shows parents how to guide their children toward meaningful friendship connections.

The I Feel Mad! Anger Workbook provides simple, actionable, and proven strategies to help kids manage angry feelings. Using this guide, your child will learn: • the rule to follow and what he or she can and cannot do when feeling angry. We discuss hat anger is a normal emotion we all have, but managing anger appropriately is a critical life skill. Your child will explore how to identify the physical sensations of anger and implement strategies before it becomes too hot to handle. The book also provides a menu of safe strategies to choose from when angry situations arise and teaches problem-solving skills and specific reactions to replace an angry response.

Also by Nadine and Donna

The I Feel Worried workbook provides simple, actionable and proven tips to help kids manage anxious feelings. In this resource, your child will learn that anxiety is a normal and sometimes necessary emotion we all experience. We discuss how to understand and label feelings including how to identify the physical sensations of anxiety and implement strategies before the fear becomes too much. There are calming exercises to choose from when anxiety-provoking situations arise as well as coping skills and specific strategies to manage anxious feelings. Your child will discover that he or she has the power to overcome anxious thoughts and become an expert worry ninja.

Being a teenager isn't always easy, and navigating friendships and relationships can be especially challenging for some teens. Our goal in writing this third book in our friendship series was to help make the social aspect of the teenage years an easier one. This time in life can feel both exciting and overwhelming. There are some challenges that every teen experiences. These include: • Changing Brains • Changing Bodies • Strong Emotions • Understanding Yourself • Developing a Value System • Awkwardness • Changing Friendships • Barriers to Social Success We know from our experience as social-emotional coaches that everyone is "friend-able." Sometimes a teen may just need a little support or advice to make that happen

Made in the USA
San Bernardino, CA
21 July 2019